CONTENTS

Any words appearing in the text in bold,
like this, are explained in the glossary.

Biographies

These boxes tell
you about the life of
inventors, the dates when
they lived, and their
important discoveries.

Setbacks

Here we tell you about
the experiments that
didn't work, the failures,
and the accidents.

EUREKA!

These boxes tell you
about important events
and discoveries, and
what inspired them.

TIMELINE

2010 – The timeline shows you
when important discoveries and
inventions were made.

BEFORE AEROPLANES

Today, many people fly in aeroplanes when they go on holiday or on business trips. Most of the world's armies have aeroplanes for fighting. People probably started to dream about flying hundreds of thousands of years ago, when they saw birds gliding through the air.

In 1783, two French inventors, the Montgolfier brothers, made the first machine to carry people up into the air. Hot air rises, so when they filled a giant fabric balloon with hot air, it lifted into the sky. This was great fun, but it wasn't the same as flying like a bird.

This early hot air balloon was launched in front of crowds in Lyon, France on New Year's Day, 1784.

EUREKA!

A duck, a chicken, and a sheep became the first living creatures to fly in a Montgolfier hot air balloon during a trial run in France on 19 September, 1783.

around 1000 BC – The kite is invented in China

THE AEROPLANE

Richard and Louise Spilsbury

www.raintreepublishers.co.uk
Visit our website to find out more information about Raintree books.

To order:

☏ Phone 0845 6044371
🖹 Fax +44 (0) 1865 312263
🖳 Email myorders@raintreepublishers.co.uk

Customers from outside the UK please telephone +44 1865 312262

Raintree is an imprint of Capstone Global Library Limited, a company incorporated in England and Wales having its registered office at 7 Pilgrim Street, London, EC4V 6LB - Registered company number: 6695582

Edited by Louise Galpine and Laura Knowles
Designed by Philippa Jenkins
Original illustrations © Capstone Global Library Ltd 2011
Illustrated by KJA-artists.com
Picture research by Mica Brancic
Originated by Capstone Global Library Ltd
Printed and bound in China by CTPS

ISBN 978 0 431118 43 7 (hardback)
15 14 13 12 11
10 9 8 7 6 5 4 3 2 1

ISBN 978 0 431118 50 5 (paperback)
16 15 14 13 12
10 9 8 7 6 5 4 3 2 1

British Library Cataloguing in Publication Data
Spilsbury, Louise.
The aeroplane. -- (Tales of invention)
629.1'3334'09-dc22
A full catalogue record for this book is available from the British Library.

Acknowledgements

We would like to thank the following for permission to reproduce photographs: Alamy Images pp. **11** (© INTERFOTO), **14** (© Marka), **25 bottom** (© George Impey); Corbis pp. **9** (© Reuters), **18** (© Hulton-Deutsch Collection), **19** (Bettmann), **26** (epa/© Hyungwon Kang); Getty Images pp. **8** (Science & Society Picture Library), **12** (Time Life Pictures/Mansell), **13** (Science & Society Picture Library), **20** (Time Life Pictures/ J. R. Eyerman), **24** (US Navy/John Gay), **27** (AFP Photo/ Aero-News Network/Jim Campbell); Jon Linney p. **7** (http://firstflight.open.ac.uk); Photolibrary pp. **4** (Science Photo Library), **15**, **16** (Tips Italia/Antique Research Centre), **17** (Imagestate/Art Media), **21** (De Agostini Editore/DEA Picture Library), **23** (Hemis/ Alain Felix); TopFoto p. **10** (The Granger Collection, New York).

Cover photograph of a Wright biplane at Helena, Montana State Fair reproduced with permission of Getty/Hulton Archive.

We would like to thank Ian Graham for his invaluable help in the preparation of this book.

Every effort has been made to contact copyright holders of material reproduced in this book. Any omissions will be rectified in subsequent printings if notice is given to the publisher.

Lifting up

Making a machine that can fly like a bird is difficult because of the different **forces** acting on it. A force is a push or a pull.

Gravity is a force that pulls everything down towards Earth. **Lift** pulls things upwards. For an aeroplane to get up into the sky, the lift force must be greater than the gravity force.

Thrust is a force that moves things forwards. **Drag** pushes against things that are moving, and slows them down or pushes them backwards. For an aeroplane to move forwards when it is in the sky, the thrust must be greater than the drag.

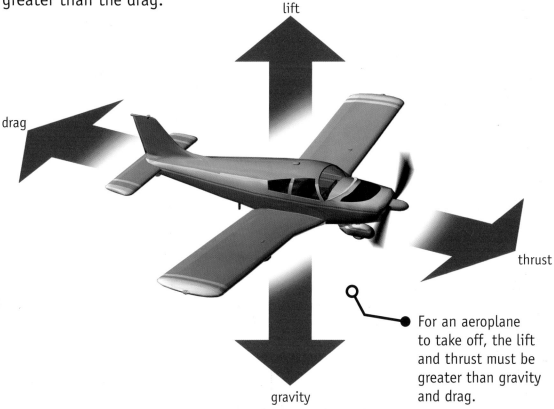

lift

drag

thrust

gravity

For an aeroplane to take off, the lift and thrust must be greater than gravity and drag.

around 1500 – Artist Leonardo da Vinci draws designs for flying machines

1783 – First flight in a hot air balloon

THE FIRST FLYING MACHINES

In 1809, English scientist George Cayley became the first person to explain how the curved shape of a bird's wing helps to create **lift**.

Wing shape and lift

When a wing moves through the air, it cuts the airflow in half. Some air travels above the wing, some air travels below it. The air going over the top of a curved wing has to go faster to keep up with the air flowing below the wing because it has further to go. When air moves faster, it has less pushing power. When air on top of the wing is pushing less strongly than the air below, the wing is pushed upwards.

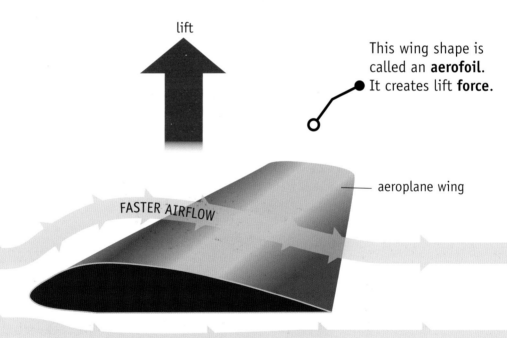

lift

This wing shape is called an **aerofoil**. It creates lift **force**.

aeroplane wing

FASTER AIRFLOW

SLOWER AIRFLOW

1804 – George Caley builds a 1.5m long model glider

1809 – Cayley publishes a book explaining important facts about flight, such as how wing shape creates lift

1800

1810

Setbacks

In 1843, Cayley designed an aeroplane with engines, but the only **internal combustion engines** available at that time were too dangerous because they used gunpowder as **fuel!**

Cayley's glider, the *New Flyer*, had wings made of long sticks with fabric stretched over them.

The first glider

In 1853, George Cayley used his discoveries about the shape of birds' wings to make the world's first **glider** that could carry a fully-grown person. A glider is a light aircraft that flies without an engine. To get the glider into the air, it was pulled down a slope so its wings were angled downwards. As the glider raced downhill, air was forced under the wings, creating more and more lift until the glider was able to take off.

7

George Cayley *(1773–1854)*

George Cayley was born in Yorkshire, England. As a child he was fascinated by flight and when he grew up he became a scientist. He made many sketches and models of flying machines, including a 1.5-metre (5-foot) long model **glider** in 1804. At that time, most inventors thought aircraft would need flapping wings to fly. By watching seagulls, Cayley realized that wings of the right shape could get enough **lift** to glide.

Cayley invented many things apart from gliders. For example, he invented a telescope, and caterpillar tracks for vehicles like tractors. After seeing one of the first rail crashes in Britain, he also invented a cowcatcher. This was a metal frame at the front of a train that cleared the track ahead of it.

This modern copy of Cayley's *New Flyer* helps to show what it would have been like to fly in an early glider. In this photograph, the glider has only lifted a little way off the ground.

Landing problems

Cayley was too old to fly his own glider in 1853, so he told his coachman to do it. To make the glider take off, a team of men used ropes to pull it down a steep slope. The aeroplane glided for some distance, but then crashed. When the coachman climbed out of the wreckage, he quit his job, saying to Cayley: "Please, Sir George, I wish to give notice. I was hired to drive and not to fly."

Better gliders

German engineers Otto and Gustav Lilienthal continued Cayley's work. They experimented with **gliders** that had flapping wings and others with two wings. Otto did most of the flying and he learned to bend and turn the wings to control the direction that the gliders flew in.

Otto and Gustav Lilienthal
(1848–1896 and 1849–1933)

When Otto Lilienthal (left) and his brother Gustav were young they experimented with wings by sewing real bird feathers together. When they grew up, they built a hill on open land so Otto could fly their gliders off it in all directions. Otto made more than 2,000 successful flights, before dying after a glider accident in 1896. After Otto's death, Gustav worked on wing-flapping aircraft, but he never managed to make them fly.

1849 – First successful glider flight carrying a person, the 10-year-old son of one of George Cayley's servants

Here, Otto Lilienthal is making a test flight, watched by a crowd near Berlin, Germany in 1892.

The next step

A glider can only stay in the air for a short time because **drag** slows it down until it stops and has to land. For an aircraft to fly forwards, it needs a strong **thrust force** to beat drag. In 1874, French navy officer Félix du Temple built an aircraft with a **steam engine**. Ten years later, Russian inventor Aleksandr Mozhaysky built a similar aircraft. The engines made steam that turned **propellers** to push the machines through the air. However, both aircrafts were too heavy and neither managed to fly properly!

Setbacks

After rolling down a long ramp, Mozhaysky's heavy machine hopped for a short distance, then hit the ground and broke its wings. Mozhaysky was uninjured. He gave up trying to fly but continued to research air propellers.

1853 – Cayley invents a glider that can carry a fully-grown person

1860

THE FIRST AEROPLANES

The first real aeroplane took to the air in 1903. The *Wright Flyer*, built by the American Wright brothers, flew for only 12 seconds but the invention changed the world. The Wright brothers had made the first powered flying machine that could take off and be fully controlled in the air.

The *Wright Flyer*

The *Wright Flyer* was a light wooden **biplane** with two fabric wings on each side. Car engines were too heavy to use, so their mechanic Charlie Taylor helped them to build their own petrol engine made of aluminium, which is a strong but light metal.

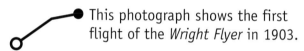
This photograph shows the first flight of the *Wright Flyer* in 1903.

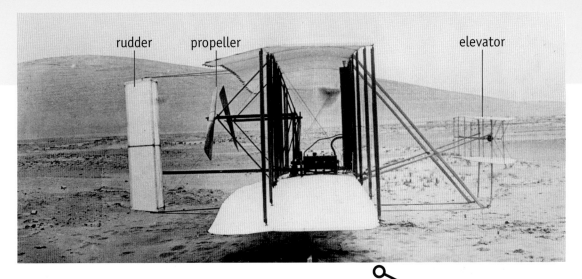

rudder   propeller   elevator

How it worked

The engine on the *Wright Flyer* turned two **propellers**. Propellers have metal blades shaped like **aerofoils**. When they spin, they pull the aeroplane forwards just like its wings lift it upwards.

This photograph of the *Wright Flyer* shows its propeller, rudder, and elevators.

To control the aeroplane, Orville pulled cables attached to the wings and **rudder**. By twisting the wings and turning the rudder slightly one way or the other, the aeroplane rolled right or left. By using a lever to tilt flaps at the front of the plane, called elevators, the aeroplane moved up or down.

Setbacks

Wilbur completed two longer flights than Orville had made, but on his third flight, the plane became damaged. As the brothers were carrying it back to be repaired, a strong wind blew the aeroplane over and destroyed it.

EUREKA!

On Orville's first flight he flew for 37 metres (120 feet) before landing safely. Although this wasn't a long distance, it was a huge achievement.

13

1874 – French navy officer Félix du Temple tries to make an aircraft with a **steam engine**

14

1884 – Russian inventor
Aleksandr Mozhaysky
attempts flight in a
steam-powered aircraft

Wilbur and Orville Wright *(1867–1912 and 1871–1948)*

The Wright brothers' interest in flying began in 1878, when their father came back from a business trip with a gift of a rubber band-powered helicopter. The boys immediately began to make copies of it. Their interest continued as they grew up and while they ran a printing business from 1890 and a bicycle shop from 1892.

They studied the work of other aircraft inventors and did experiments with kites and **gliders**. From 1900 to 1903, they made and flew a number of gliders to discover how a plane could be controlled. After 1903, they made and tested many more planes, and by 1905, the latest *Wright Flyer* could turn figure-of-eight shapes in the sky.

The Wright brothers tried to sell their invention to governments around the world, but at first people thought they were crazy. Finally, in 1908 they started to make and sell aeroplanes for buyers such as the United States Army. They went on improving their aeroplanes and displaying them to crowds of people. In New York in 1909, a million amazed spectators watched Wilbur fly. The brothers became celebrities.

A bat-winged plane

After the Wright brothers' success became known, French inventor Clément Ader claimed he had made the first powered flight. He said he had flown on 9 October 1890, in a steam-powered, bat-winged **monoplane**, which he named the *Éole* (pronounced "ee-ol"). There was never any proof that Ader had flown.

This photograph shows Clement Ader's aircraft, the *Éole*.

15

1891 – German engineer Otto Lilienthal is the first person to make safe, repeated gliding flights

Going further

In 1908, the *Daily Mail* newspaper in the United Kingdom offered a prize of £1,000 (about £100,000 in today's money) to the first person to fly across the English Channel. On 25 July 1909, French inventor Louis Blériot's **monoplane**, the *Blériot XI*, made the crossing in just 36 minutes. Blériot's engine was less powerful than a modern scooter's, but it carried his wood-and-cloth plane safely across the 35-kilometre (22-mile) stretch of water. After his famous flight, Blériot started an aeroplane business, building more than 800 aircraft by 1914.

Setbacks

Many people thought French pilot Hubert Latham would be the first to cross the Channel, but on two attempts the engine of his plane stopped working and he crashed into the sea.

Here the *Blériot XI* can be seen making the first flight across the English Channel.

1903 – The Wright brothers make the first powered flight in the *Wright Flyer*

1905 – The new, improved *Wright Flyer* can be fully controlled in the sky

1908 – Wright brothers start to make and sell aeroplanes

1908 – Alfred Wilm creates duralumin, a new metal for making aeroplane parts

1900   1910

World War I aeroplanes

During World War I (1914–1918), aeroplanes became weapons of war. At first, armies only used planes to spot where enemy troops were on the ground. Some pilots began to take guns up with them to fire at targets. This led to the invention of new fighter planes. These planes had machine guns attached to the front to shoot down enemy aircraft.

EUREKA!

In 1908, German inventor Alfred Wilm created a new metal. Duralumin was a mix of aluminium and other metals, and it was very strong but very light. The Germans kept the discovery a secret during World War I, when they used it to make German fighter planes.

This British bomber plane has been shot down in France in 1917.

1909 – Louis Blériot's monoplane, the *Blériot XI*, makes the first crossing of the English Channel

AEROPLANES TAKE OFF

During the first part of the 1900s, aeroplanes flew higher and further than before and the first passenger planes were built. The Douglas DC3, invented in 1935 by American Arthur Raymond, was the first aeroplane to carry enough passengers to make a profit. Engine noise inside was reduced by having thick carpet on the cabin floor and rubber around the engines.

The Douglas DC3 made flying comfortable and quieter for the 24 passengers it carried.

EUREKA!

More people wanted to fly after reading about the record-breaking flights of pilots such as Charles Lindbergh and Amelia Earhart. Lindbergh made the first **transatlantic** solo flight in 1927, and Earhart became the first woman to fly across the Atlantic alone in 1932.

1927 – Charles Lindbergh's first transatlantic solo flight

1928 – World's first air ambulance service starts up

Air ambulances

Doctors had long realized that aeroplanes could carry people to hospital in emergencies, such as during wars. The first successful **air ambulance** service, called the Flying Doctor service, was set up in 1928 in Australia, where many people lived far from a hospital. Most air ambulances today are helicopters, because these can take off and land **vertically** in places planes cannot go, such as rooftops. The large blades above a helicopter's body are shaped like **aerofoils**. When they spin, they create **lift** and the helicopter takes off.

In many of the first air ambulances, patients were strapped to the aeroplane in their stretchers.

EUREKA!

The first truly successful helicopter was the VS-300, built by Russian-American engineer Igor Sikorsky in 1939. The small blades at the back of the helicopter turn in the opposite direction to the big blades to stop the helicopter body spinning round.

1932 – Amelia Earhart is the first woman to fly across the Atlantic Ocean alone

1935 – Flying boat *China Clipper* makes the first flight across the Pacific Ocean

1935 – **Radar** is invented

1939 – World's first successful helicopter is invented

1939 – First turbojet-powered aeroplane flight

Flying boats

In the 1930s and 1940s, rich passengers travelled in flying boats. These were aeroplanes designed to land on and take off from water. The planes had boat-shaped bottoms or **floats** on the wings, so that they would not sink. A flying boat named the *China Clipper* made the first flight across the Pacific Ocean in 1935. Some flying boats were huge, with bedrooms, dining rooms, and lounges!

Howard Hughes
(1905–1976)

American Howard Hughes was a multi-millionaire and plane fanatic who set many aeroplane speed records. In November 1947 he built the giant, eight-engine *H-4 Hercules* flying boat. With its wingspan of 98 metres (320 feet), it was designed to carry 750 passengers. Hughes flew it once for a short distance, but it was too heavy to fly properly.

Howard Hughes' *H-4 Hercules* is landing on water after its first and only flight.

1940–1941 – Germany uses aeroplanes to drop bombs over the United Kingdom

1947 – Chuck Yeager breaks the sound barrier in the world's first **supersonic** flight

1947 – Howard Hughes builds the giant, eight-engine *H-4 Hercules* flying boat

World War II planes

Aeroplanes played a very important part in World War II (1939–1945). Bombers were big planes with several engines and large **fuel** tanks so they could travel long distances to drop bombs. Fighters were made of light aluminium metal so they could be quick and move easily in sky fights against enemy planes.

Attacks by German bombers on Britain in 1940 were known as the Blitz.

British fighter pilots were guided towards their targets by new **radar** systems. Radar was invented in 1935 by Scottish scientist Robert Alexander Watson-Watt. By sending **radio waves** into the sky and studying the echoes that bounced back when those radio waves hit an object, command centres could locate enemy aircraft and tell pilots their position by radio.

JET PLANES

The invention of the turbojet engine greatly increased the distance and speed that aeroplanes could travel.

How turbojet engines work

A turbojet engine sucks air into the front part of the engine. A **compressor** squeezes the air into a **combustion chamber**, where **fuel** is added and burnt to create hot gases. Some of these hot gases turn a **turbine**, which works the compressor. The rest are blasted out of a nozzle, creating the **thrust force** needed to push the aeroplane forwards.

This diagram shows how a turbojet engine works.

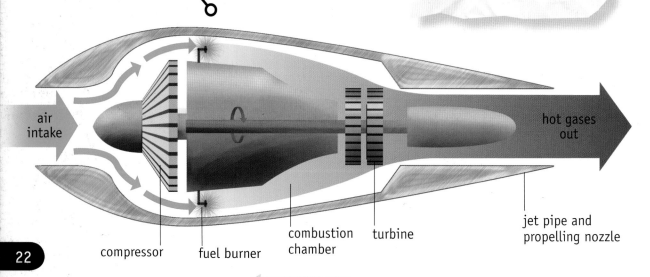

air intake

hot gases out

jet pipe and propelling nozzle

compressor   fuel burner   combustion chamber   turbine

direction of aeroplane

1966 – Harrier jump jets are developed

1970 – The first jumbo jet, the Boeing 747, enters passenger service

1960

1970

Jet airliners

Airliners are jet planes that carry passengers. The first jet airliner was the de Havilland Comet in 1949. It could fly at 800 kilometres (500 miles) per hour and carried 36 people. Bigger and faster jet planes were built as more people wanted to travel abroad for their holidays. **Jumbo jets** are giant airliners that can carry huge numbers of passengers. The first jumbo jet, the Boeing 747, flew its first passenger service in 1970, and it could carry about 350 people.

EUREKA!

In 2005, a new double-decker superjumbo jet with seating for about 500 people took its first flight. Airbus A380 is so big that there would be room to park 70 cars on its wings!

The Airbus A380 is the world's largest passenger plane.

23

1976 – Concorde is the first **supersonic** jet to operate a passenger service

Breaking the sound barrier

In 1947, American pilot Chuck Yeager became the first man to fly at **supersonic** speeds. At the height that aeroplanes fly, sound travels at about 1,100 kilometres (700 miles) per hour. When a plane goes almost as fast as sound, it catches up with the **sound waves** travelling in front of it. It squashes them together into a barrier just in front of itself. When a jet breaks through this sound barrier, the squashed air spreads out suddenly. When this shock wave hits the ground, people hear a sonic boom – a noise like a giant clap of thunder.

EUREKA!

In 1976, Concorde became the first supersonic jet to operate a passenger service. It could fly at Mach 2 – twice the speed of sound.

This is the moment a supersonic jet breaks through the sound barrier.

1989 – First test flights of stealth bomber aeroplanes

This is a U.S. Air Force stealth bomber.

Jet fighters

Over time, armies have developed different kinds of jet fighter planes. Harrier jump jets were invented in the 1960s by British engineer Sydney Camm. Harriers can jump straight up into the air when side engines are aimed downwards to thrust the jet up. Stealth bombers were developed in the 1980s. These planes are shaped to reduce **radar** reflections and made of materials such as radar-absorbing paint. This lets them sneak up on targets without being spotted by enemy radar systems.

Sydney Camm
(1893–1966)

Sydney Camm trained to be a carpenter but was fascinated by model planes. He became an aeroplane designer in 1923. He designed many planes, including the famous Hawker Hurricane fighting planes of World War II, but the Harrier jump jet was his last.

Harrier jump jets can take off **vertically**!

25

Today, buying an aeroplane ticket is cheaper than ever before and there are a huge number of planes travelling across our skies. This isn't good news for everyone. Some people are protesting about new runways being built on areas of countryside, and others worry that aeroplanes use too much **fuel** at a time when oil is running out and that burning fuel makes air **pollution**.

New designs

In the future, more planes may be made of lighter materials such as carbon fibre, which would use less fuel. New designs will create more **lift** once planes are moving through the air. Future planes may also be powered with **renewable** sources of energy, such as solar power, rather than oil.

Solar cells on this plane Helios, which first flew on solar power in 2001, convert the energy in sunlight into electricity to make it fly.

26

2003 – First flight of Helios, a solar-powered aeroplane

2004 – SpaceShipOne is the world's first private aeroplane to fly to the edge of space

2005 – The world's first superjumbo, Airbus A380, takes to the air

Space planes

In the future, passenger planes may also fly to new destinations, such as the Moon! Early spaceships were transported into space by rockets, which could only be used once. In 1981, a space shuttle was launched into space like a rocket but it landed back on Earth like a plane, ready to be used again. Some engineers think that future space planes may be run by high-powered jet engines.

Could ordinary people be taking flights into space in the future, on aeroplanes like SpaceShipOne?

EUREKA!

In 2004 American businessman Burt Rutan's SpaceShipOne became the first private aeroplane to fly 100 kilometres (60 miles) above Earth to the edge of space.

TIMELINE

around 1000 BC
The kite is invented in China

around 1500
Artist Leonardo da Vinci draws designs for flying machines

1783
First flight in a hot air balloon

1804
George Caley builds a 1.5m long model **glider**

1908
The Wright brothers start to make and sell aeroplanes

1905
The new and improved *Wright Flyer* can be fully controlled in the sky

1903
The Wright brothers make the first powered flight in the *Wright Flyer*

1908
German inventor Alfred Wilm creates duralumin, a new metal for making aeroplane parts

1909
Louis Blériot's **monoplane**, the *Blériot XI*, makes the first crossing of the English Channel

1927
Charles Lindbergh's first **transatlantic** solo flight

1966
Harrier jump jets are developed

1947
Howard Hughes builds the giant, eight-engine *H-4 Hercules* flying boat

1947
Chuck Yeager breaks the sound barrier in the world's first **supersonic** flight

1970
The first **jumbo jet**, the Boeing 747, enters passenger service

1976
Concorde is the first supersonic jet to operate a passenger service

1989
First test flights of stealth bomber aeroplanes

1809
Cayley publishes a book explaining important facts about flight, such as how wing shape creates **lift**

1849
First successful glider flight carrying a person, the 10-year-old son of one of George Caley's servants

1853
Cayley invents a glider that can carry a fully-grown person

1891
German engineer Otto Lilienthal is the first person to make safe, repeated gliding flights

1884
Russian inventor Aleksandr Mozhaysky attempts flight in a steam-powered aircraft

1874
French navy officer Félix du Temple tries to make an aircraft with a **steam engine**

1928
World's first **air ambulance** service starts up

1932
Amelia Earhart is the first woman to fly across the Atlantic Ocean alone

1935
Flying boat *China Clipper* makes the first flight across the Pacific Ocean

1935
Radar is invented

1940–1941
Germany uses aeroplanes to drop bombs over the United Kingdom. This is known as the Blitz.

1939
First turbojet-powered aeroplane flight

1939
World's first successful helicopter is invented

2003
First flight of Helios, a solar-powered aeroplane

2004
SpaceShipOne is the world's first private aeroplane to fly to the edge of space

2005
The world's first superjumbo, Airbus A380, takes to the air

GLOSSARY

aerofoil curved part of an aeroplane's wing that helps it fly

air ambulance special aircraft that carries patients to hospital

airliner large plane that carries passengers

biplane aeroplane with two sets of wings, one above the other

combustion chamber part of an engine in which fuel is burned

compressor machine that squashes air or other gases

drag force of air that pushes against objects

floats light objects that float in water

force push or pull that makes things move in a particular way

fuel material that produces heat or power

glider light aircraft that flies without an engine

gravity force that attracts objects in space together. Gravity pulls things towards the centre of Earth.

internal combustion engine engine that produces power by burning fuel inside it

jumbo jet large aeroplane that can carry several hundred passengers

lift upward push of air on an aircraft as it flies. Lift is a kind of force.

monoplane aircraft with one set of wings

pollution something that makes air, soil, or water dirty

propeller device with two or more metal blades that turn quickly

radar method of spotting distant objects using radio waves

radio waves form of energy that moves through the air

renewable something that will not run out. Renewable energy is energy generated from natural resources, such as sunlight, wind, and waves.

rudder flat blade that sticks up at the back of a plane and turns the plane left and right

solar cell device that changes energy from sunlight into electricity

sound wave vibration in the air caused by sound

steam engine engine that produces steam to move parts, usually by burning fuel

supersonic faster than the speed of sound

thrust force produced by an engine to push a plane forwards

transatlantic across the Atlantic Ocean

turbine machine with a set of blades that spin when driven by steam, gas, water, or wind

vertically straight up or down

FIND OUT MORE

Books

Amelia Earhart, Tanya Lee Stone (Dorling Kindersley, 2007)

Flight, Richard Platt (Dorling Kindersley, 2006)

Flight: From Icarus to Space Ship One, Penny Clarke (Book House, 2007)

Websites

To find out more about the Wright brothers go to:
http://www.wright-brothers.org

Find out more about the history of flight at:
www.ueet.nasa.gov/StudentSite/historyofflight.html

Learn about aerodynamics at:
http://firstflight.open.ac.uk/history/index.html

Places to visit

Flight Gallery, Science Museum
London SW7 2DD
www.sciencemuseum.org

Imperial War Museum
Duxford, Cambridgeshire CB22 4QR
http://duxford.iwm.org.uk/

National Museum of Flight
East Lothian, EH39 5LF
www.nms.ac.uk/our_museums/museum_of_flight.aspx

INDEX